From Pavilion to Parkinson's

Spiderwize
Remus House
Coltsfoot Drive
Woodston
Peterborough
PE2 9BF
www.spiderwize.com

A CIP catalogue record for this book is available from the British Library.
The views expressed in this work are solely those of the author and do not
necessarily reflect the views of the publisher, and the publisher hereby
disclaims any responsibility for them.

ISBN: 978-1-912694-64-8

FROM PAVILION TO PARKINSON'S

MANDY HOY

SPIDERWIZE
Peterborough UK
2018

I am going to dedicate this book to Ross Foulds. This may seem strange, as I have never met this person and do not know him. This gentleman works with Himmy and brought a copy of the original book I had printed myself, just for friends and family. I let a few people I know, read this book and they all said it was brilliant, but friends and family say that, especially to someone who is ill. Now Ross didn't know me, so had no reason to be generous with opinions, but he was, very generous. In fact, he gave me a brilliant review and if it wasn't for his review I would never have gone ahead and printed the book for general sale. So Ross that is why the book is dedicated to you and the lovely Amanda, thank you both.

Contents

Introduction

I can never remember not being afraid as a child, to us it was normal, we thought everyone's dad was violent like ours, until we went to school.

According to my mum, the first time my dad really slapped me hard, after losing his temper, was when I was 6 weeks old and was messing about with my bottle. Knowing what I know now I am surprised, he didn't cause any brain damage or worse. My mum said I never cried after that when he was at home, so even at 6 weeks old, I knew when it was safe and when it was not.

To be honest, there are lots of gaps in my childhood memories, I have been told it is normal for the brain to suppress such memories. I have been offered help to open these up, but as my brother, who unfortunately for him remembers every minute, has told me what I forget, I don't think I will ever be ready to recall everything and cope.

Sometimes odd memories come back with such clarity, they are very upsetting. The most recent one, was just after my brother got married and we were at my cousin's birthday party. She is 13 years older than me and I she was talking about how she and her husband met, all those years ago and how different it is now.

I was a bridesmaid when they got married, only 5 years old, I remember a lot of people repeatedly say smile, smile and I can remember holding my breath, as I didn't know how to smile. Imagine 5 and not knowing what a smile was. I did manage to take one photo where I looked happy, but my poor brother looks terrified. Smiles were few and far between until I was 13 and my brother was 10. When we eventually escaped, we were homeless for a couple of months, sofa surfing, always split up, as no one we knew could accommodate all of us together. So my mum and my brother went together to a friend's house and I went to my aunty Do-do's, with my aunt Gladys. Aunty Gladys lived with us after my little grandma passed away, as she was epileptic and never married – in those days epilepsy was viewed very differently to today.

My mum tried to get us a house, but in those days it was very different, she didn't have custody for a start and as her name was still on the house she shared with my dad and he had not been paying the rent and was in arrears, they wouldn't even consider it. Fortunately my aunt already had her name down and eventually she got a 2 bedroomed flat and we moved in with her.

I remember a long time after we'd left my dad, myself and my brother were coming out of the school gates to walk home and we heard a man's voice shouting our name, as my dad had spent months trying to locate us, we grabbed each other's hand and just ran for our lives. It wasn't him it was our uncle John my mum had 2 sister's Do-do (John's wife) and Gladys he realised we had assumed it was our dad and he felt awful bless him. He'd just seen us walking and thought he'd offer us a lift, an innocent thing to do, little did anyone realise the damage that had been done.

We both felt our real childhood began when we left our dad and although we had nothing materialistically, we didn't care because we had peace, happiness and a life without fear.

My mum

15 and innocent
Wandering what life had in-store
Will I have a family?
Travel or so much more

I want to tell her story
What cards fate dealt to her
What the future held
It is now time to share

On a blind date she fell in love
He swept her off her feet
Suave, funny and handsome
A paratrooper, she did meet

Doing national service
Things were perfect as could be
Writing sending photographs
Working hard in a factory

Saving every penny
For the perfect start
She'd really fell in love
And promised him her heart

Sadly things were not as perfect
When they settled down you see
For behind the handsome exterior
A monster hid beneath.

Beatings all the time
Put down frequently
Too scared to open her mouth
Slowly losing her identity

One dream she held onto
Was children of her own to bear
Someone to hold and cherish
Someone to hold and care

But fate again was very cruel
After 10 long years of waiting
Pregnancy brought only heartache
After another fatal beating

At the 9th hour a nurse let slip
You poor little thing
You must be devastated
By the news the doctors bring

Then it dawned on her
The reality was there
Inside her the daughter she'd dreamed of
And would soon have to bear

Was so disfigured and ill
She'd died at the 11th hour
And empty cot at the bottom of the bed
A wasted baby shower

A year later and now a son
But again fate said no
A kick to her stomach
Dealt his heart a fatal blow

He struggled for 2 days
He tried so hard to hang on
But God saw him suffering
And the next thing he was gone

Now I could not even begin to guess
Or ever imagine how that would feel
My mind cannot start to go there
How would you try and deal

A year later and more joyful news
But this pregnancy did not bring
A smile, joy nor happiness
As her heart forgot how to sing

The beatings continued
Worse than ever before
How could anything survive?
How would this child be born?

But this baby was different
She was as determined as she was tough
No amount of beating
Would ever be enough

Yes that daughter you've guessed it
Who was so bloody minded was me
A miscarriage later
A little brother I would then see

Now the years that followed were harsh
No let-up was there for her
But there were colours in her rainbow
From the children whom she loved and cared

Eventually she got out
With only the clothes she had on
But this didn't bother her
As long as she protected her daughter and son

Now even though life wasn't easy
She still struggled every day
But nothing ever stopped her
And not once did she dismay

She never let her children down
She stood firmly by our side
Sharing pearls of wisdom
And through our dark days she would guide

Then grandchildren came along
And my God what a Nan
The best there ever was
This made up for the years with that man

She thrived and she grew
Life once again she enjoyed
Holidays and picnics
With her 2 girls and her boy

But fate didn't let up
Many strokes did she endure
50, 60, 70 they lost count
They're were many more

Although these took their toll
They never stopped her having fun
With her beloved grandchildren
Lots of holidays in the sun

So when you hear me say
I am my mother's daughter
She inspired me to be strong
You can now realise, where I'm coming from

My mum was amazing
She was the very best
No one could ever come close
She passed every hurdle, every test

I miss her every day
And still feel her by my side
My mother's my inspiration
My protector and my guide

So on this day like many
I want to pay tribute to
My mum up there in heaven
God bless mum, I'll always love you

This picture has always haunted me
This young girl I always wanted to meet
Because no cares burdened her
And the whole world was at her feet.

In memory of Madeleine and Kevin, my older sister and brother. You waited a long time to see our mum.

Love and look after her x

Looking back

I sit here so often late at night
Looking back at years gone by you see
Decisions and memories so many
Painting as it sets my mind free

From the very beginning it was hard
Not a childhood you'd relish to share
Terrified of a man, pure evil
A man never able to care

Ruled day after day by terror
No let up from violence and fear
A childhood dominated by alcohol
And a father who drank too much beer

Listening at night as he beat her
Too scared to breathe or even look
Holding onto each other tightly
Hour after hour it took

Never daring to cry, frozen like ice
Praying for the punches to stop
A silence two children learned quickly
For if they cried a beating they got

Childhood memories overcast by the dark
Coloured by an indescribable foe
Memories locked away in my mind
Where even my subconscious dare not go

13 years night after night of suffering
Then that fateful night occurred
I stood in front of my father
To protect him? Don't be absurd

With a knife in her hand and murder her intent
The last beating had been one too much
But it wasn't him I was protecting
As I knew me she would not touch

I had to protect my mother
And stop her from an act she'd regret
For a sentence she'd face for certain
If at her hands, his ending he met

Homeless for months
Walking the streets were we
But our minds were at peace
We were happy and free

I'm not saying it was easy
Life back then was so very tough
But we always had each other
And somehow this was enough

Soon into adults we grew
With families of our own
Many ups and downs we faced
Any adversity soon overthrown

But I know they're still there
In the back of my mind
Nightmare from my childhood
That I hope never to find

There's only one person left now
Who suffered long ago like me
Who is always there when I need him
He is my brother you see

And no amount of distance
Or miles of roads between us
Will ever be too far or too many
To stop that closeness because

Once a long time long ago
In the darkest of nights
We held onto each other
To overcome terror and fright

My Little Brother

I do not see him every day
Sometimes a month or three
But never underestimate
What my brother means to me!

There's one thing you should know
No matter where we are
No distance will ever be too much
And no journey will ever be too far.

In my heart he will always be
And I know I am safe in his
Because of what we went through
When we were little kids.

I remember walking on that ward
Like it was only yesterday
Looking at that little cot
Where my baby brother lay.

I helped change his nappies
And held him when he cried
I loved feeding him his bottle
And rocking him when he tired.

When we heard those footsteps stamp
Our heart jumped in our throat
We'd grab what we could carry
And run off down the road.

We'd spend hours huddled up
In the pavilion, on the park
Too terrified to go home
Often sitting there till dark

Every night the same
Mum screaming out in pain
Beating after beating
Over and over again

The terror was relentless
We thought it would never end
We'd hold onto each other
He was my only friend

Then sometimes it was our turn
The footsteps neared the door
We hide under the bed covers
In the wardrobe, or on the floor

But nothing ever stopped him
Beaten till I could hardly breathe
And when it got too much for me
My brother would scream at him to leave.

Knowing that he'd then get hit
I would just shake and cry
Watching my poor baby brother suffer
Wondering if this time, one of us would die!

Only we will know
Because only we were there
No one else will ever know
The nightmares that we share

Only we together
Remember all those years ago
The dark days of our child hood
And the evil we'll always know.

Now there are only 2 of us
Since the day we lost our mum
Just the 2 of us to remember
The horrors that long ago were done

Yesterday I stood there proud
Tears welling up inside
As I watched my baby brother
Take his lovely bride.

No one will ever understand
Or come close to even feel
The love and bond we'll always have
Because of what we had to deal

So never underestimate
Because I don't see him every day
What my brother means to me
Every minute in every way.

We would spend many days sitting huddled together in a pavilion on a park, come rain, snow or sunshine, long until it was dark and we knew it was safe to return home, after our dad had gone to work. Too terrified to go home before, even when we were hungry.

Monsters live in wardrobes

Monsters live in wardrobes
Or hide under the bed
They wait until night time
And then frighten you to death

This is the fear
That many children hold
When it gets dark
Their blood, it starts to run cold

But many years ago
I realised the truth
That real monsters live with us
Not hiding in the roof

They sit at the table
They sit and watch TV
They sit on the sofa
Alongside you and me

They're not tall and purple
They're not short and blue
They're just human beings
Exactly like me and you

Something that I learned
When I was just a child
They greet you with a handshake
And a great big smile

They lay there in your bed
Or sit right there in the chair
And every so often
Even pretend to care

But this nice person
you think that you can trust
All of a sudden
For no reason starts to cuss

They get in your face
Especially after a drink
And make you feel worthless
Control is there instinct

They need to own and rule
Have power and control
A slap or a punch
Helps them own your very soul

You end up so afraid
of everything they do
that one day you forget
Just exactly how to be you

If you are lucky
Something makes you see the light
You know there's more to life
Than living in fright

You turn your back and flee
And run for your life
This takes a lot of courage
When all you've known is strife

But with a bit of help
Someone offering a hand
It's possible to move forward
And life can once again be grand

Only one women in my life
Has ever had the strength
To walk out with nothing
And go to any length

To rebuild a life alone
To set off and start again
It takes a very strong person
Someone so very brave

I admire my mum so much
More than I could ever say
She will always be my hero
and my inspiration every day

Everlasting summer's day

As long as I remember
Every minute day or night
You always protected me
You were never out of sight

The thought you'd go away one day
And not look after me
I could not bear to think of
And hoped I'd never see

You filled my life with joy
Fun and laughter all the way
Memories of outings
On an everlasting summer's day

You shaped me as a person
Taught me right from wrong
You gently instilled your wisdom
Pushing me along

In the blink of an eye
Childhood was far behind
Marriage, work and children
We're the only things on my mind

It was not always easy
But you were always there
Showing me the way to go
Dispelling all the fear

I watched you as a grandma
And envied you so much
As my children's lives you enriched
With your golden Midas touch

It's impossible to know the pain
You hid so very well
Because you refused to give in
And would never ever tell

I looked back over the years
And remember yesterday
I still feel you with me
Like you never went away

Now feet run around me
And laughter fills the air
I am the grandma now
It's my job to be there

As I pass on your wisdom
I hope that I can be
The mother, person and grandma
That you'd expect me to be

I was struggling for about 2 years with the symptoms of Parkinson's – not knowing what was wrong, but knowing it was serious, I struggled to grip, my hands would freeze a few seconds into doing my teeth, I had a really bad tremor at times. But I, like a lot of people, I thought if I ignored it, it might go away – yes, I work on a busy social work team by trade and I do know better!!!

It took my son to drag me to my GP and force me to confront my problem. My doctor did some basic checks and said, "well it appears your brain is losing control of your body, I am unable to tell you more and will refer you to a neuro specialist at the hospital......don't worry". It is no secret, I have not got a lot of respect for a lot of doctors, consultants and a lot of receptionist......but really what a prat.

Well after 22 months I saw a consultant to be told, it's not me you want, I will re refer you to a colleague. Another 3 months of waiting and 20 seconds it took the consultant to tell me I had Parkinson's. Now 25 months waiting for anyone, let alone someone who has worked in social care for 20 years, is a very, very long time and my best friend and I "Mr Google" spent many hours looking at every neurological illness known, yes, yes I know, but, well there was no way I could sit patiently and wait, doing nothing. Now I had self-diagnosed either MS (very similar symptoms) or a brain tumour!!!! So when he said Parkinson's at first, I could have kissed him, I was relieved initially – not the reaction he was used to I suspect, as he looked very shocked. He said he would send my GP a letter telling him what tablets to give me and said goodbye!!!

The impact of being diagnosed with Parkinson's didn't hit me for about another month and then the reality of what actually was wrong with me was like a building landing on my head.

When I was diagnosed my consultant invited me to join a study for Parkinson's and looking at trauma/violence in childhood and the possibility of a connection with early onset Parkinson's.

This is what made me also write about my childhood experiences, because they were then connected.

I didn't go, I was still coming to term with my diagnosis and that was too much to take in at that time. But I often think, the man who made me suffer for the first 13 years of my life, was also to make me suffer the last years as well!

'Invisible Disability' was the first poem I wrote, shortly after being diagnosed. This was when I heard Robin Williams took his own life, thought to be due to depression at having Parkinson's. At the time I couldn't understand why, I can now.

Invisible Disability

I am a disabled person
It is a part of me.
I have not lost an arm or leg
It is something you cannot see.

I do not use a wheel chair,
Walking stick or crutch.
I have no missing limb
Deformity or such.

These invisible disabilities
Come in many different forms
And because you do not see them
We appear just like the norm.

You will not sit and listen
Or stand and offer me your seat.
You will never understand
The daily hurdles I have to beat.

Everyone assumes it is a blessing
To look like nothing's wrong.
But to keep up this illusion
Means you have to be twice as strong.

I do not understand
Why society is so ashamed.
But things need to change
So no one's alone and feels to blame.

I hate to hear when someone
So desperate and alone.
Takes a drastic action
Instead of picking up the phone.

But until we open up our ears
And look and try harder to see.
These illnesses will remain invisible
And no one will know but me.

My suit of armour, I wrote when my symptoms first began to get really difficult to cope with, it was one hell of a shock. I was newly diagnosed and felt I had to be seen to be positive and show how well I was coping. Even when I was terrified.

My Suit of Armour

I wear my suit of armour
Which no one else can see
It starts off with a smile
And an anecdote or three

I cannot begin to tell you
The fear I feel inside
The absolute terror
That I strive so hard to hide

Will it take me quickly?
Or will it take me slow
How will it affect me?
The doctors just don't seem to know

I take my medication
To help me through each day
How long will it last this time?
Even the specialist cannot say

Each morning is a struggle
Fighting pain that is so bad
Every step is a night mare
But I won't let it keep me sad

I will not let it beat me
I try hard never to be down
With angels all around me
I rarely wear a frown

I don't know what the future holds
Or what trials I will have to face
But hopefully I will always count my blessing
And accept it with good grace.

The first lot of medications, only lasted 6 months and then the symptoms got out of control again and I needed more medications to stabilise me. It was then I realised, whatever they gave me, would only stabilise me for a short while, before I got used to it and needed an increase or an adjustment. I then realised I would never recover, feeling good would always be short lived and I was slowly getting addicted to these drugs and was totally dependent on them. Something that had always scared me.

Also by this time, I had watched my poor mum die, on her death certificate "Parkinson's complicated by Pneumonia". She also suffered arthritis all over, had 60 – 70 TIA's, cancer, was partially sighted and had hearing impairment. She cared for all her grandchildren and her great grandchildren at times and was always present, always there and always putting her children first. You can see why this amazing lady was my inspiration.

My children and granddaughters are also a massive part of my life and my love for my granddaughters has saved my life, as they are my reason for getting up every day, carrying on and surviving the terrors and darkness of the night.

What does the future hold?

What does the future hold?
What is to become of me?
What does life have in store?
How hard is it going to be?

Every night when I'm alone
This is what goes through my head.
Will it be so difficult
That I'll wish that I was dead.

Will I be able to show the same strength?
That my mum showed to me.
Am I the woman?
That she brought me up to be.

I pray every night
For the strength to carry on
And thank God for the angels
He sent to keep me strong.

God bless my son and daughter
They make me feel so proud
They are my own creation
I want to stand and shout.

Then there are my girls
Like stars shining up above
Filling my days with fun and laughter
And un devoted love.

Then my rock and strength
A man who has managed to change my life
By giving up everything
And asking me to be his wife

God make me worthy of the love
That these angel's bestow lovingly
And give me the strength
to face the path opening up in front of me.

And Lord when I stumble
And to the ground I fall.
Hold my hand and lift me up.
For I'll need you most of all.

Although I am not massively religious, I do believe in God and have felt his strength, when I have prayed to him. I suppose like most I do only speak to him when I need help, but occasionally I do remember to thank him.

Andrew

Andrew come here,
Andrew get out of there
Andrew get of that hedge
Andrew come eat your veg

Andrew behave
Andrew do that
Andrew get down that tree
Andrew don't torment that cat.

Andrew do this, Andrew do that
For years that's all I said
Andrew your name was always on my lips
And never out of my head

Then you went silent
Fighting for your life
Terrible times were upon us
Nothing but fear and strife

Sitting by that hospital bed
Nothing to do but stare
Holding your hand tightly
Saying a little prayer

You had a guardian angel
Who was watching over you
And slowly you improved
And took a step or 2

You went from strength to strength
And soon you were back
Andrew don't torment your sister
& remove that noose from around her neck

Then you went to school
I missed you such a lot
My blond haired little cherub
My special little tot

Over the years I watched you
A boy turned into a man
Ice skating, taekwondo, scouts
And a massive Forest fan

A loyal apprentice
Worked hard as hard can be
Then one day he became
An engineer on a CNC

He likes his flash cars
And his lovely lake side flat
Spending times with family
Watching sports and that

I cannot explain
Or ever begin to say
How proud I am of the man
Who stands before me today

Andrew come here
Andrew go there
Andrew can you do this
Andrew can you do that

I am the nuisance now
How things have turned around
How much we have changed
Life is so profound

I not only love you
But I am so very proud
Of the man I have raised
And I want to shout this out loud

"This man is my son"
"and I am as happy as can be"
"to have such a devoted son"
"who looks carefully after me

I just want to thank you
You have enriched my life
By just being you
And never bringing strife.

Nichola

We used to laugh and chat
Even when you were in my womb
I knew your every thought
Like you knew my every mood

Even during labour
You knew I'd suffered enough
Spending months beside a hospital bed
So you birthed yourself with one easy push

I held you in my arms
And looked down upon your face
Such beauty and dignity
Such defiance and grace

We cuddled every morning
When you'd slip into my bed
I'd tuck you in at night
With your favourite little ted

A pretty little angel
As good as good can be
A lovely little chatterbox
Always sitting on my knee

A brother she looked up to
Her best friend was he
She loyally looked out for him
And held onto him lovingly

She always had an answer
She always knew best
She was always the first to hear gossip
And never failed to test

Determined with a strong will
Liking the last word
Teenage years were never boring
Telling tales, some quite absurd

You were always your mother's daughter
When I looked at you I'd see
A lot of myself in there
No one to blame but me

And although we had our battles
I was always by your side
And when you said "help me mum"
It was on me that you relied

I watched you have my granddaughter
I've never been so proud
I stood on every street corner
And shouted this out loud

Then dark days were upon me
And my little girl had gone
A woman in her place
Pushing me gently along

Every sneaky trick she'd learned
Every devious thing she'd done
She used it to save my life
She was so very strong

It was then I found my best friend
We knew each other well
Someone to love and laugh with
And secrets I could tell

A challenge I now face
A battle I now have to fight
With my best friend by my side
I know I'll be alright

A love I cannot measure
And the way I feel inside
When I look upon your beauty
My chest swells up with pride

Because my best friend is my daughter
It was me who helped her grow
Into a daughter to be proud of
Someone I'm honoured to know.

TT

Toyah the dancing queen
Toyah the queen bee
Toyah you are very sharp
You are so much like me

Sensitive and kind
Clever and smart
You like your own way a little too much
But you have a massive heart

I love the time I am with you
I hate you not being here
I enjoy the things we do together
And the secrets that we share

Like you I miss the past
When it was just me and you
Sleeping in my bed
Adventures just us two

Playing in the park
Picnics on the grass
Feeding ducks and swans
Sunny days that flew so fast

Although these times are over
I'll remember them like you
They are our special memories
We'll cherish, no matter what we do.

Zena

With a shy little smile
She puts her head around the door.
She sidles up beside me
And says "hello mama".

Can I have a huggle?
Can I sit upon your knee?
Such a lovely little girl
Always showing her loyalty.

As you get to know her
And the person that she is.
You admire the effort
That goes into that first kiss.

She's happier in the background
Modesty she prefers.
An intelligence she hides
Accolades she defers.

She never demands her own way
She is happier to go,
Along with the majority
She never makes a show.

She worships her big sister
An admiration plain to see.
A devotion so clear
And an obvious loyalty.

But there is also another side
Which comes as a surprise.
Just try and bully her
And you see her mother's eyes.

That beautiful little smile
Has captured my heart.
I love all the huggles
And hate when we're apart.

Zena I would like to says
Thanks for all you've taught me.
Especially how to smile
When facing adversity.

*L*ate at night in bed after listening to colleagues talking, I decided to try a dating site, even messages would break the loneliness and darkness at night. I was lucky enough to meet the most wonderful man. Things got serious very fast, not a minute to spare when you are ill. He soon became my rock and started to repair my life.

POF

I was all alone,
Fed up and feeling blue.
So I decided to go fishing,
It seemed a good thing to do.

What should I use for bait?
What do I want to catch?
I was feeling very greedy,
So I wished for a perfect match.

I chose my bait carefully,
And put it on the hook.
I sat and waited patiently,
Wonder if I'll have any luck.

Did I want a nomad?
007 or huggy bear?
They all sounded so pretentious.
It made me very aware.

Then a "night in white",
With a smile of pure gold.
Caught my line and took the bait,
Onto him I longed to hold.

It was a little battle,
As he turned to get away.
So I gave him a little line,
and plenty of play.

Then I had him hooked,
This time he was all mine.
And now one thing I know for sure,
He is my for ever Valentine.

The Norse God

Evil was all around
Dark days were here
Then upon the horizon
The Norse God did appear.

A red flag on his back
And a puffer in his hand
Strong and tall he stood
As he surveyed all the land.

I will not be beat
Every battle will I fight!
I will conquer all
With my heart and my might.

He took the beast by the horns
A battle did ensue
But the Norse God prevailed
As his heart was pure and true.

But the battle took its toll
And wounds did he sustain.
His health suffered badly
And he couldn't hide the strain.

The fight was nearly over
The battle almost won.
Everyone in the land
Admired what he had done.

Now he sits in his castle
With his maiden dear.
Good times lay before them
Happiness is here

I'm thankful every day
For what the Norse Gods done.
As my life is now perfect
As my heart the Norse Gods won.

Knight in white

Dark skies were everywhere,
When will they ever go?
Bad luck over whelmed me,
For how much longer I did not know.

Then onto the horizon,
A knight in white suddenly appeared.
He stood strong and firm,
No evil did he fear.

Goodness was his shield,
Honesty his lance.
Sat on a faithful steed,
He made the devil dance.

He turned the evil tide,
He made the world seem bright.
Him and him alone,
Turned the dark to light.

When the fight was over,
And he'd banished all that was bad.
He held me in his arms,
And said come don't be sad.

He turned around and spoke,
Sit on the back of me.
And I will love you forever,
From now to eternity.

He carries me everywhere,
I am never, ever alone.
My defender, my protector,
My guardian, my home.

All my fear has now gone,
And the darkness hides away.
With my knight I'll remain forever,
Until my dying day.

And as I take my last breath,
One thing I won't forget.
The happiness I've experienced,
Started the day when first we met.

The repair man

I know a repair man
He's a laid back kind of guy.
I met him 2 year ago
When he came into my life.

He surveyed things with his puffer
And his trusty cup of tea
Let me see now what needs doing
Leave everything with me.

He started on the garden
he cleared out all the shed
A tin of paint and a scrubbing brush
And a new mattress on the bed.

Up and down from Manchester
He put in many miles
Fitting in a kitchen
And lots and lots of smiles.

Holidays and meals out
He never ever stopped
Where does he get the energy
Let's get those trees chopped.

The living room and bedroom
The landing and the stairs
The attic and a dressing room
Do I really live here.

A fence and some decking
Now a roof and guttering
A walk in shower in the bathroom
And much decluttering

Wow how much have we accomplished
Look at what's been done
All inspired by the repair man
My heart he's definitely won.

He took a lot of pieces
And fixed them up a treat
And put me back together
Now my life is so sweet

Thank you Mr repair man
Thank you very much
for all the magic you've performed
And your finishing touch

Himmy

I never imagined that I would find…..
Or even dared to dream.

I wouldn't believe….
In a million years.

A man would treat me like a queen.

But one day on the internet…..
I saw a lovely smile.

Charming and a gentleman…..
His messages had style.

Eventually we agreed to meet…..
With baited breath I'd wait.

He drove all the way to Nottingham….
This would be our first date.

After what seemed like forever….
And ever and a day.

A car pulled up on my drive…
We didn't know what to say.

A gentle giant stood before me….
With a smile I'd never seen.

In a Metro link uniform….
All smart and pristine.

Soon conversation flowed…
Like I'd known him all my life.

Many thousands of miles later…
He asked me to be his wife.

Now I am aware…..
What John means to everyone.

I know that you will miss him…
As soon as he has gone.

But to all up North….
and his family so dear.

I promise you I'll love him….
And with you all I will still share.

Because Nottingham not far away…..
As long as I physically can.

I am happy to make sure…….
You see this very special man.

And last but not least….
I just want to say.

Thank you Tina L'Estrange….
For your advice to John that day!

My Northern hero took me on a whirlwind of holidays, trips to the theatre, concerts and shows, he wined and dined me and we had weekend away, life was wonderful for a while, but like always it's short lived. He took the big gamble of moving south to be with me, left everything and everyone he loved to try and save me. Something he regretted several times after!!!

What was once
so perfect

What was once so perfect
What was once so pure
Is now unclear
And I'm no longer sure

My knight in shining armour
Now no longer holds me tight
I lay alone in bed
Thinking about once was so right.

Will I go to work one day
And come home to find you gone
do you still love me
Or are your feelings done.

I can't imagine life without you
I can't see how I'd go on
I want to wake each morning
Knowing I'm the only one.

Nothing last forever
that's what people say
everything has to end
everything has its day.

Without you I am empty
I'm only half complete
Can we make it right again
Can life go back to being sweet

I can only hope and pray
This will all blow over and pass
And we'll return to normal
With nothing damaged or dashed

Because you hold my heart now
I trusted it in your care
I hope you take care of it
And don't leave me in fear

Dashed hope

From day 1
I relied on you
Never any doubt
You'd see me through

You spurred me on
You gave me hope
For the first time
I knew I could cope

But that's all gone
Now I can't rely
You've destroyed the image
Of the caring guy

Sticks and stones
Are easily forgot
But what leaves your mouth
Is somehow not

There was a time
I had no doubt
You'd be by my side
And with me you'd shout

"You'll never win"
"You won't beat us"
Now I stand alone
As I no longer trust

You to be that strong
You to be there
I no longer see you
As someone who cares

My knight has gone
I no longer see
A hero
Standing in front of me

I am unsure
I don't know how I feel
My emotions are all over
You're no longer real

I now know
I stand on my own
And at the end
I will be alone

But I'm not giving in
I know I am strong
I will fight to the end
And I don't need anyone

It'll be just me
But I am prepared
And when it's my times
I won't be scared

I will face this fight
With or without you there
With a quiet dignity
And no more fear.

Then a massive blow, another chronic condition, it wasn't my Parkinson's, I was having awful pain in my knees, an unrequired cartledge operation, set off chronic Osteoarthritis, apparently my bones were now going soft.

After 6 months of suffering and a holiday and another drug increase, meant a short lived but miraculous recovery.

Hitting home

It's really hitting home now
It's really getting tough
One chronic conditions hard
But 2 was proving too much

Just when I think I'm on top
And everything's settled and right
Another hurdles thrown my way
Another battle to fight

I need to find the strength
The will power to go on
A drive never known before
Now more than ever I have to be strong

Two conditions to control
And both medications conflict
Either stay in control of Parkinson's
Or get rid of the sticks

More than ever now
I need angel's here on earth
Cos the love I hold for them
Is everything I'm worth

I look in the mirror
And my mum looks back at me
It was a surprise at first
But now all at once I see

God blessed me with the tools
Everything I need to go on
As I am my mother's daughter
Stubborn, tenacious and strong

And with the love I have around me
Although the war I cannot win
I have enough fight to do battle
For now and not give in

So bring it on I'm ready
I will put up one hell of a fight
Mentally I'm prepared
A stronger me is insight

I know Parkinson's can't be beaten
I don't expect a miracle cure
But now I'm prepared again
Let battle commence once more.

I needed my angels, my granddaughters more than ever. I have many times loved the way children see things and tend to smile and not get concerned about serious illness, they just get on with it and think I want to play!!! So that became my motto.

My babies

Skipping along
Arms waving in the air
7 year old
And not even a care

Oh with upsets sometimes
That seem oh so much
But with a daddies protection
And a mummies loving touch.

Her life is so wonderful
Magic and pure
No one on earth
Could ask for much more

Then there's her big sister
Makes us all proud
Baking wonderful cakes
As light as a cloud

Self-taught on the flute
Music she can read
Just past her music exam
Yes, very proud indeed

Then there's her S.A.T's
Oh what a star
Over 100% in all
These girls will go far.

My Angels on earth
On them I do rely
To lift me up higher
Way up into the sky

Inspiration I draw
And the strength to go on
Every day is a battle
Which for them so far I've won

Dark days are here
Battle weary am I
Ground down to my knees
I silently cry

But I will not give in
I will continue to fight
With every breath in my body
And all of my might

I've too much to live for
I've too much to do
I can't let it beat me
I will see this through

I want to skip
With my hands in the air
Just enjoying the day
For once, without a care

War

The time has come
The war is near
Sword in hand
Armour ready to wear

Now I am prepared
I feel ready now
Years of preparing
So I know how

To take this fight
To the next level
I'm ready now
To dance with the devil

I'm feeling calm
I'm feeling strong
I now know what to do
Bring it on

Battle plan sorted
I'm ready to go
Has it attacked my heart
It's too early to know

My immune system
Is also under attack
Onward and forward
And no looking back

Finances in order
Loved ones aware
Palace adorned
Chariot in gear

My foot soldiers ready
My mum by my side
Bring it on Parkinson's
It'll be one hell of a ride

" **H**ow much more can I take", you think to yourself? Then new hope, in the form of a physio and manager of the Parkinson's NUH rehab unit at the City hospital in Nottingham "Christine".

I was introduced to her one day and I admire her so very much. I showed her the Warrior poems and I don't think she was very flattered. I meant them to be a huge compliment, as she is one of my hero's now. She is tough and drives everyone, staff and patients alike. She has self-discipline, like I have never before seen before and I love the fact that she puts the fear of God into all the doctors and consultants.

Warrior the beginning

I'd lost hope
Nearly given in
Held my hands up
Looks like you win

Day by day
Inch by inch
Every step unbearable
Pain it made me wince

Every hope
Every prayer
Bloody mindedness
No longer got me anywhere

All the love
I had around
No longer inspired me
I was so down

I always thought
I'd do better than this
To go on many years
Was my only wish

Give me strength
To God I'd pray
Help me Lord
Through one more day

Then I asked
And was introduced to you
Who said all angels
Were sweet as dew

Butter wouldn't melt
With an innocent look
Pleasant manner
Scribbling in a little book

Och my dear
Oh woe is me
Is that the best you can do
So you've got a bad knee

Tuesday morning
Prompt at 8
Bring plenty of water
And don't be late

Too scared to argue
Or to disagree.
But very slowly
That painful knee

Started to improve
A little more each day
No instant miracle
But in a steady way

Dare I hope
Dare I believe
Could this be the
Inspiration I now need

Will this work
Will I improve
She gave me hope
And picked up my mood

It won't be easy
It'll be very tough
It's up to you
It's going to be rough

I'll try my best
I'll do all I can
It's in my hands again
And how much I can stand

Thank you Christine
I know it's what you do
But this is my life
And I've got hope again Thank 2 you .

Warrior – It's begun

Two soldiers by my side
We'll fight this war with you
two soldiers standing firm
We know a trick or 2

Don't give up do not despair
We won't let you give in
We have some magic weapons
And we can teach you how to win

Slowly and patiently
Techniques I learn to use
I know it won't be easy
But I can win if I choose

I woke up this morning
And said a little prayer
God help through 1 more day
And the pain enough to bear

I put my foot down on the ground
And slowly I stood up
Am I dreaming?, I dare not hope
As the first step that I took

Hardly any pain
No swelling on my knee
I walked into the bathroom
Can this really be

There was still the usual tear
Welling up inside my eye
But no longer with the pain
But a tear of joy I cried

For the first time in a long time
I know that I can cope
The soldiers with their magic
Have just given me new hope.

I'm a warrior now

Warrior training
Is moving along
I'm a warrior now
And I'm getting strong.

My walking stick
I can lie down
A smile has replaced
The tears and frown.

A new attitude
Has come over me
From my negative ness
I now am free.

The harder I push
The stronger I get
I won't let up
I've a long way yet.

But I'm back on top
And I won't give in
Once again
I feel I can win.

Looking back
To that fateful day
When I'd given up
And you came my way

Then my rock, the man I relied on had a haemorrhagic stroke, I will always blame myself and the burden he tried to carry.

My own health dropped rapidly after that and although he recovered, I didn't.

The pressure on both of us started to show, I had to pretend even harder and make out I was fine.

I'm back

I'm back
I'm ready
Bring it on
As long as I have you I'm strong

I may not have stood
And made any vows
But I'll stand loyally by you
Any old how

You gave up everything
Just for me
And I will look after you
Just wait and see

I'm in my comfort zone
When my backs against the wall
This is what I'm used to
So I know that I won't fall

I will sort this
We will be fine
Place yourself in my hands
And give me time

I've spent my life
Learning how to survive
It's now second nature
Learning how to stay alive

I like the challenge
That's when I'm at my best
Just you sit back
And get plenty of rest

Because I need you better
And waiting for me at home
I can cope with anything
But not being alone

For the first time in a long time
I am back to being me
Someone I haven't been
In an absolute eternity

So here I am
I am strong
Stand back and watch me
Because now the battle's really on

My Prayer for Himmy

One by one Lord
you've challenged me
Each hurdle I overcame.
With grace and dignity

Whether a child, a teen
or a young mum
Each battle I fought
Until it was won

You took my Childhood
And scarred my teens
the supposedly best years
Were never seen

Then the dark years
When I nearly lost my son
Battle weary
But you still weren't done

Then on holiday
You struck again
My strength was tested
But it never waned

Then my health
You took away
I faced new challenges
Every day

But I conquered them
because I had the strength of two
A guardian angel
Sent by you

He picked me up
When I was down
Carried me
When he saw a frown

He's my everything
He's my every day
I lean on him
In so many ways

Now he needs me
And I will be there
I'll carry him
Every day I swear

Please let him live
Please leave him here
Please oh Lord
Hear my prayer

Well Himmy you won your war

Well Himmy
you won your war
And once again
Your standing tall

But I am battle weary
A casualty on the floor
I did not do as well
And am struggling once more

But it was a massive risk
one I had to take
And given the same circumstance
This decision I'd still make

Because you are now
The one on who I will always depend
Through all my darkest days
Me you have to mend

You won't let me give in
You push me hard to fight
I know with you behind me
I'm going to be alright

So come on be my rock
Bend down and I'll climb on
Well fly away together
Off into the rising Sun

Soaring high

Soaring high,
In a beautiful sky
Weaving through the clouds
No one there
Not a care
Only an engine roaring so loud

Come with me
Come hold my hand
I show you things
Like Egypt's sand

The pyramids
We'll sail the Nile
Watch the sun rise
I'll make you smile

Then volcanoes
In Tenerife
Snorkelling
Along a beautiful reef

Gay Paris
And the Eiffel tower
Arc de triumph
the louvres beauty
forget the hour

Theatres. Plays
concerts or show
Dining and dancing
Off to the cinema we go

Anything you want
I'll try and provide
A caravan, a car
So you're safe when you drive

A hundred miles
That's not far
Id fly around the world
For someone too share

Someone to hold
Someone to love
Someone to be there
When life gets tough

But while we can
Come with me
There so much more
For us to see

We're off again
We're on our way
To where once upon a time
The Gods did play

Then who knows
What is in store?
Italy, Rome, Australia
Or more

Come on Mandy Hoy
And don't look back
Don't give up
Do not crack

Come with me
Hold my hand
The world is ours
And life is grand

You're a man of your word
That is true
I feel invincible
When I'm with you

Side by side
You fight with me
Battling an enemy
You cannot see

You give me strength
And all I desire
So we're here again
Flying higher and higher

In the clouds
High above
Just you and me
And our eternal love.

I now realise my babies were becoming young ladies and play time was nearly over, for the first time I had to apologise to Toyah, never did I think I'd take my fears out on her, my life, my everything.

The world is yours Toyah

Proud and straight
Tall and True
A young lady
Through and through.

Intelligent,
does well at school
My TT,
ain't nobody's fool.

Don't try to argue
Or disagree
She'll leave you standing
Just you wait and see.

But there's also,
Another side.
That from most people,
She tries to hide.

She learnt to control these demons
And banish these negative thoughts
And as her confidence grows
She is now a lot less fraught.

An I.T bod like her dad
Computers her middle name
She finds them very easy
And puts most others to shame.

She has another skill
On the flute she is self-taught.
She looked it up on Google
Everything was there she sought.

Her music is divine
She is a pleasure to listen to,
A talented child by far
With anything she decides to do.

Then there is the baker
She is now quite the cook.
Her cakes are the best
And they taste as good as they look.

But most important of all
Is her big sister role
A little mum she is
Sometimes she acts so old.

Some days I sit and look
At the young lady she has become.
Her natures like her father
But a face just like her mum.

Her emotions she cannot hide
And with a look she will let you know
You've taken a step too far
Push no more, turn around and go.

I miss my little girl
But I've enjoyed watching her grow.
I loved our time together
And see her confidence glow.

The world is your oyster
TT, great things you will achieve
Because you are determined
And have lots of self-belief

I am proud to sit and watch
And enjoy being there
To know she is my granddaughter
And she loves me so dear.

Summers nearly over

The sunny days of my childhood
We're over cast with a dark cloud
But later on, becoming a mum
Allowed me to play and run around

But all too soon those days were over
As my children grew
But soon a miracle happened
And I was blessed with you

Once again I played
Shouted and ran around
Paddling, feeding ducks and playing
Games like dobby of ground

And then along came another
This was a dream come true
We were the three bandits
Toyah, me and Zu

If there was adventure we'd find it
And experiments we loved to try
Painting, baking and lots of crafts
Made each day with my girlies go by

Now I can see this childhood ending
As I sit and watch you grow
It makes me very sad
Cos I don't want it to go

I love to play so much
I enjoy going on the park
I never really grew up
I suppose cos my own was dark

The last days of my childhood
Are now coming into sight
I won't have anyone to play with soon
Or to act silly with or fight

I am getting older
and my health is getting bad
I will miss childhood games
It makes me feel so sad.

No more summer days
Autumn will soon be here
Soon I'll have to grow up
And this is the one thing I really fear

No more building sand castles
Soon there will be no time to play
I suppose everyone has to grow up
And put their toys away

But until that day is here
I will make the most of my last days of play
And then I will sit and watch the sun set
And goodbye to my childhood say

This was the day I dreaded the day I realised I had become a burden, words cannot say or describe how much I hate that!!!

Thank you daughter

I could not do this
without you
there's no way I could face this
The way I do

To get out of bed
Every day
And face the world
Come what may

Everyone's hero
It makes me grin
Cos I'm not brave
I know I can't win

Once you've come to terms
With what is your fate
you have to make the most of things?
before it's too late

You motivate me
To enjoy myself
And help to do things
While I've still got my health

You make me laugh
And you're ready with a cuddle
You sort me out
When I get in a muddle

Simple things
like a cup of tea
Or a secret treat
Just for me

We have our moments
Just like anyone
But as soon as they're said
Then It's over and done

You come and help me
Every day
You never moan
Even though you have no time to play

I could not do this daughter
without you
Thank you baby for every day
you help me through

Toyah – You were my very being

From the moment you drew breath
And I set eyes on you
A love so overwhelming
Swept over me and I knew

I would always love you
And want to keep you near
To watch and help to guide you
And take away the fear

You were my first best friend
As we spent many hours together
I loved every minute with you
You were my forever

I proudly watched you grow
And loved you so very much
Your Beauty was astonishing
As was your magic touch

You were my inspiration
My one and only drive
Through many dark hours
Your smile kept me alive

I love to see you happy
And would give you anything
I'd offer you my last breath
If you needed it to sing

I would give my life
Without a second thought
As into my life such happiness
You have always brought

This is a dark day
One I hoped I'd never see
When I had to hurt you
And know it had to be

Because I love you so much
I feel so much pain inside
And for every tear that falls
A little part of me dies

You are my very being
You are all I live for
I want us to get through this
And be best friends again once more

I hope you still love me
And I hope we'll be able to make amends
And once more become
The very best of friends

Zena – my hero, my light

When you were born
And I looked at you
An overwhelming love
Now I had two

Looking very similar
But not the same
Because of the whole world
You were afraid

We held our ears
When we took you out
Cos all you did
Was scream and shout

Your big sister
Was the only one you'd trust?
If mummy wasn't there
Then Toyah must

But as I watched you grow
And saw you fight
Your determination
Was out of sight

A quiet little soldier
But a soldier no less
At war with fear
She had no rest

Diabetes
And a perforated ear
Not one sign of self-pity.
Or despair

You were an example
To us all
Your kindness and forgiveness
Had me in awe

I've never met some
Quite like you
But you are my hero
My little Zu

Recently I have got a lot worse and I think at times, how much more can I take, then I see my children and well, I think hopefully as much as Parkinson's can throw my way.

One last fight

Once more I'm struggling with my mobility
This is a massive blow
I am putting up one last fight
Before I let it go

I am exercising day and night
And have arranged all my doctors to see
If this does not help now
Then what will be will be

I will lose this fight eventually
There is nothing I can do
But I won't be beat easily
One hell of battle will ensue

A wheelchair is daunting
But if it's the only outcome
Then that's what I will do
Be sure I am not done

While I can draw breath
One thing you can be sure
I won't be beat easily
As to me there is so much more

My daughter my carer

When your children
Look after you
It's not right
It's not what they should do

I see my baby
All worn out
I hate myself
I just want to scream and shout

But no matter what I tell her
Or what I say
She runs around
And visits every day

I can manage
It just takes me longer
And with these injections
I should get stronger

Please oh lord
If not for me
But for my baby
Sort out my knee

I can't stand
To see her worry about me
So help me now Lord
And give her some peace

Will it work?

Waiting to try something new
Apprehensive once again
Cos if this treatment fails
It means a life of permanent pain

I don't know how much longer
I'll be able to carry on
How will I suffer the pain?
And stay mentally strong

Before now it's been easy
Because I've always had some hope
But how do I come to terms with this
And how do I cope

Lord give me strength
To deal with what comes next
I need your strength inside me
To overcome this test

Thank you Lord

Thank you Lord
Once again
It's not a miracle cure
But it's eased the pain

This means I can cope
And it gives me new hope
And once again it's up to me

It back in my hands
I can once again stand
And there's a whole new possibility

Now I can move forward
The war with Parkinson's can resume
And my warrior head
I can now assume

But I couldn't do this Lord
Without you by my side
Holding my hand
And being my guide

And when it got bad
I felt you lift me up
You carried me
And let me drink from your cup

Now once more
The fights back on
I'm still at war
But this battle now can be won.

A Coping cake

A teaspoon full of knowledge
And a tablespoon of hope
A cup or two of bravery
All go together to help you cope

Mix it all together
In a great big pan
Add as much love into it
As you possibly can

Then kneed it all in cuddles
And wrap it up in prayer
Leave it to stand a while
And then your nearly there

Cover it with determination
And some bloody mindedness
Trim it with some passion
And limit the amount of stress

This is the recipe
That you will need to bake
If you are to stand a chance
And a successful war to wage

The quantities aren't important
But the ingredients are
And if you have them all
Then they will take you far

Am I afraid?

Am I afraid?
Of course I am
How do I cope?
I gather all the strength I can

Did I think?
Did I realise
How hard it would be
All the rivers I'd cry

No I didn't
And I still don't
Cos if I stop and think
Then carry on I won't

But every day
The Strength I must find
To get out of bed
And leave the dark thoughts behind

Each day the sun rises
Whether you like it or not
And giving up
Won't make that stop

Flowers will still bloom
And winds will blow
Seas will crash
And crops will grow

And everyday
I will get up and strive
To be the best I can
And stay alive

Am I afraid?
Well wouldn't you be
What will tomorrow bring
I'll just have to wait and see

My Daughter

She always has time
She's always there
With so much patience
Showing how much she cares

I tend to say things
I've already said
She listens intently
And never corrects

She's comes to see me
Every day
And talks on the phone
For hours I'd say

She's helped me to walk again
Just like I did her
She washed me and dressed me
And tidied my hair.

When I have a bad day
she's always at hand
straight to my side
helping me stand

I watch her so proudly
whether at work or at play
She grown up so beautiful
in every way

A mum and a wife
Always on the go
Jogging, doing hair
She's doesn't know slow

She is my daughter
And my best friend
She's always there
And someone I can depend

Being a mother
The hardest job I know
But my proudest achievement
With the love they now show

Thank you my daughter
For everything you do
For my beautiful granddaughters
And for just being you

Once upon a time

Once upon a time
A long time ago
Santa was real
And at Christmas there was snow

The tooth fairy visited
And left money under a pillow
We loved Andy Pandy
And watched wind in the willows

Happily ever after
Was how the stories ended
No one died
And everyone got mended

This never worried me
As into adulthood I grew
I left these myths behind
And problems were few

But now I face uncertainties
And my future is unsure
I need to believe
In these miracles once more

I want a happy ending
I need this to be true
Cos I'm afraid of what the future holds
I haven't got a clue

Do you believe in magic?
Do you think there's a chance?
That this pain and madness
Will disappear per chance

Well it is a nice thought
But not likely to come true
As happily ever after
Is now long overdue

Work has always been important to me and I have loved every day I've worked for Social services – 20 years in one role or another. I have some wonderful bosses who have been amazing at supporting me and a brilliant employer – which I have to thank for bending over backwards keeping me at work.

My work keeps me sane, it stops me feeling sorry for myself and every day I go out and help someone and go home thinking, how lucky I am!!! I think of it as saving the world...... 1 person at a time.

My career spans 20 years

My career spans 20 years
Every day doing a job of care
Working hard helping others
Fathers, sons, sisters and mothers

Saving the world
One by one
Improving lives
That's hopefully what I've done

A privileged job
And I feel blessed
I've loved every day
And give it my best

Social care
It's all I've done
It now keeps me sane
Now I'm the needy one

But every day
It teaches me
How lucky I am
Compared with most I see

I learned long ago
To be grateful for
Whatever I have
And not to want more

Cherish life
Keep loved ones near
Help others if you can
It's nice to show you care

Put a smile
Or wipe a tear
Take time out
to show you care

Then hopefully
One day far away
All your good deeds
Will get repaid

And someone will come
And Extend their hand
And light the way
And help you to mend

We are taught
Everything you share
Is repaid tenfold
So help others and care

Now it's no secret that I hate computers and am useless with them, it's my generation I suppose, then again it quite possibly could be me.

LL

I hate my computer
as I struggle with I.T.
Why can't they make it easy?
For an idiot like me

I didn't like "Carefirst"
But with"Castle" I did my best
But now there's "Liquid Logic"
Now this I really detest

Notes not observations
Action plans, no messages
Notify and watch it
I'm always in a mess

But I have a hero
She always helps me out
When I'm cursing and swearing
And throwing things about

She's steps in and saves the day
And makes everything seem clear
Thank you Mandie
You really are a dear

E ven now as ill as I am, I cannot let an opportunity to push or promote a good idea pass me by and CTS (Community Together Surgery) is just that. It puts Social Workers back where they belong, accessible and in the community, working jointly with other community groups and I am glad to be a part of a group of SW's working to make this a reality in Nottingham. I was honoured because the Nottingham City Social Service head decided to use this poem on their road shows.

CTS

We all share one world
under the same Sun
we breathe the same air
and in the same dirt we run

some lives are easy
some lives are not
that's why it's important
to share what we have got

there are different religions
but all say the same
be good don't hurt others
and in death you will gain

different tongues
speaking different words
different clothes
from all over the world

some come from where its hot
some from where it's cold
some from countries so poor
to where we have riches untold

some people flee from war
to find a better life
some people for no reason
find themselves in trouble and strife

There are the hungry and the poor
and those who are mentally ill
other struggling bereavement
and those addicted to pills

there's the old and the frail
the isolated and lonely
some with sensory problems
to name a few only

so come where you are welcome
where you'll find help and a smile
come tell us your problems
we'll go that extra mile

We'll put you in touch
with some community support
try and help reassure you
and leave you less fraught

Come seek us out
at the community together surgery
we have a selection of biscuits
Juice, coffee and tea

5 minutes or an hour
stay as long as you choose
come search us out
you have nothing to lose

It has always annoyed me, how people treat the down and out. I have found over the years, there is always a really tragic story behind these poor people's misfortune.

The Invisible

Walk right past,
don't speak to me,
pretend I'm invisible,
someone you cannot see.

I've not always been this way,
in a very distant past,
I walked among society -
life was fun and fast.

I may not look the norm,
I have a bottle in my hand
and I talk to folk you cannot see
and live rough on the land.

I have not lost a leg,
or bare a visible scar,
my wounds are deep inside my mind,
my sanity's at war.

I have no diagnosis,
no one knows what's wrong.
Why? Because I'm invisible
and my mind has gone.

I missed out on education,
no one bothered to send me to school
and as I have no learning -
I am treated like a fool.

Even if I hadn't slipped through the net
and a someone had asked what's wrong.
I don't know how to put into words,
what I've suffered with for so long.

The voices are my only friends
and days are long and hard,
time has no meaning,
neither does light or dark.

So use your compassion
and take a little while,
it only takes a minute
to say good morning and smile.

Treat me like a human being,
just give it a try.
Think to yourself I'm lucky -
there but for Gods good grace go I.

But for now I'll remain invisible,
someone you pretend not to see
and society will remain ashamed
and keep on ignoring me.

How can we have advanced so far
and not really moved at all.
Where is the safety net,
to save us when we fall?

One day my pain will be over,
one day I will be gone,
no one will even cry or mourn me,
when I have moved on.

Because I am invisible
and folk choose not to see,
because they do not want to know,
but there are lots of me!

Do not criticise

Do not sit in judgement
you don't know what I've seen
do not make your mind up
until you've been where I have been

Life is not been easy
at times it's been very rough
you cannot begin to imagine
how I suffered, life's been tough

Not everyone is lucky
A rose garden it is not
there was no perfect childhood
schooling I never got

It easy to be smug
and criticise what I've done
you sit there in your ivory tower
life for you is a bundle of fun

You never stop and listen
or give me the time of day
you walk past very quickly
go rapidly on your way

I am society's problem
That they brush over to one side
don't bother to try and deal with me
it's easier if I hide

When I die no one will mourn
I won't ever be missed
no father to look up to
no mother to tenderly kiss

Next time you see me about
try taking the time of day
just a smile or nod
say hello, go out your way

You might just be surprised
you will never know
you might find I'm quite nice
go on try, give it a go

Just don't sit in judgement
don't look down on me
be grateful you're not in my shoes
it's easy, try and see.

I am often asked questions by colleagues at work, about my illness and I say "I'm doing fine" or "I'm brilliant" It's a lie of course, but you can't spend all day self-pitying, when you are there to help others.

What's it like

What's it like
How do you feel
Are you scared
How do you begin to deal

These are questions
Everyone wants to know
I see it in their eyes
Even though they try not to show

Yes I'm scared
I'm really terrified
And for most of the time
From the truth I hide

I do not think
Or attempt to deal
With my illness
I try to pretend it's not real

But now and again
It overwhelms me
I get afraid
About what will be

Already
I've started to lose
The ability
to do what I choose

I cannot walk
It affects how I talk
And in a short while
It'll take my smile

I'm incontinent
With this I struggle
I worry if I smell
When we're close and cuddle

Often I can't control
Or use my hands
I struggle to sit up
And often can't stand

I see the pain in my
Loved ones eyes
This more than anything
Makes me cry

So I make a joke
And put on a brave face
Laugh at my clumsiness
And lack of grace

These fears and terrors
Are now mine to hide
There's no one now
That I'm able to confide

What will happen
What will become of me
All I can do
Is wait and see

And try to struggle on
One day at a time
And try to convince everyone
That I'm doing fine

It's a lonely place
And a difficult fight
The darkness is spreading
And out is going the light

I was diagnosed in 2013, June 6th, but the physio reckoned I have had Parkinson's 8 to 10 years. I was suffering a good 3 or 4 before I was diagnosed.

In my job role I was asked if I wanted to not do cases with neuro issues in them, I said no, I had already nursed and seen my mum's journey with the illness, so there weren't many surprises. I have thus met many fellow suffers and the ones with a good sense of humour and low stress levels seem to do the best. I think this is the case with any illness, or in fact life itself. Easier said than done I'll be the first one to admit. Keeping occupied and being able to help others is the other ingredient to my sanity, along with my lovely family.

When I started my journey and I first experienced pain, I look back and see how bad I thought I was. But it was easy compared to now and I can only assume, now will be easier than in another 2, 3 or 4 years. They have said there is a good chance, when I deteriorate enough for me to have the brain operation, which is supposed to be very effective and good, this gives you about 10 more years and then you can start the medications again, as they are usually able to slowly reduce you dose, when you have had the implant.

It's not all bad news apparently chocolate is recommended for Parkinson's and red wine!!!! Every cloud has to have a silver lining!!

Dual with the devil

The devil whispered in my ear
Just watch while I break you
I turned around and began to laugh
that's one thing you'll never do
Cos wo betide,
with my army by my side
I will put up one hell of a fight
And it's very rare
that I ever scare
especially when I know I'm right
Bring it on
I'm prepared and strong
I'll do whatever it takes
I'm ready now
I'll show you how
you'll see how a hero's made
So come and dance
Take a chance
Devil if you dare
But think on this
Watch whatever you dish
cos one day I might end up down there

Stop and smell the flowers

We take so much for granted
Each and every day
Rushing around getting things done
Never taking time to play

Now this year I've have learned
To stop and smell the flowers sweet
To get up and greet the morning
And the sunrise meet

I do not worry about money
Not that I have a lot.
But I work on the assumption
I can't spend what I haven't got

I don't get burdened down
When someone says something I don't like
I get on with my life and think
It's there problem not my strife.

I remember a favourite aunt of mine
Who in my heart I hold so dear
She taught me how to count my blessings
And let go of hatred and fear.

Now these lessons didn't mean too much
Until I had to face
The fight of my life against an illness
That challenged my dignity and grace

Now I cherish every cuddle
Every opportunity I have to play
With those nearest to me
Who I love and see everyday

I now realise
That we only get one try
We come this way once only
Before we have to say goodbye

I try not to waste a minute
I will make sure I enjoy
Spending quality time with family
And not worry about what I cannot buy

We will eat and drink too much
And old fashioned games still play
We'll talk and laugh for hours
And appreciate our holidays

And I will greet every day with determination
And steal myself for the fight
But I'll take time out to smell the flowers
And appreciate the stars at night

Blessings and good wishes
Keep those you love near
I hope you got all you desire
And may peace replace any fear

We started having problems again, John and I and this time I thought we would split, things became very, very tense, poor John this is not what he signed up for. I have changed so much as a person and deteriorated so much and I have found it very difficult to know and cope with myself – how he managed I will never know. This period lasted many months and I feared we would not make it at times, but after many ups and down and much soul searching, on both sides, well we're both together and happy, for now and planning a trip to Australia – that could be a whole book on its own – if I survive!

It's all over

It's all over
I did it again
I took his love for granted
And caused him pain

I cannot expect
Or even deserve
One more chance
For him I've hurt

He's been my everything
All this time
And now I'm devastated
He's no longer mine

He's carried me
For all these years
And now I have to accept
He won't be here,

How will I go on
How will I survive
How will I move forward
Where will I find my drive

Without his good night kiss
Gently on my face
Without his strong arms
Wrapped around my waist

Never lying beside him
Ever again
Life will never ever
Be the same

Saying sorry
isn't enough
It's way too late for that

He's moving on
It won't be long
Then he'll be in his own flat

Even though I love him
I have to let him go
My illness is too difficult
for him I know

Now God more than ever
Please be here by my side
Cos now on my northern giant back
I will never again ride

Good bye my love,
You were my world
My one and only chance

Now the end feels near,
You no longer care
The devil's waiting for his dance

Talking to Kim

Why is it easier to talk to Kim
Someone so far away
It's because she doesn't see what I've become
She doesn't remember me that way

Pity doesn't come into it
Just an honest opinion
She made me think and made me see
The answer to my question

When did I stop enjoying us?
And stop showing you my love
When did I shut you out and why?
It's just become clear because

Someone across the other side
In Australia far away
Took time out and made me think
Why I'm behaving this way

I read my poems, my journeys track
To when I started to wear a mask
To when I started to shut you out
It wasn't an easy task

When we were speaking, it all made sense
Why didn't I see it before?
How could it not occur to me?
A light bulb moment for sure

Remember when returning home
The first time I needed help
You wanted to get a wheelchair
And I insisted on doing it myself

It's just occurred, what's wrong with me
Why was that so bad?
How come I was fuming?
What made me so mad?

Playing with the children
And when I'm at work
Both times I'm in charge
God I'm such a jerk

I struggle letting go
Not being in charge
Let someone push me in a chair
I'd rather give it the large

I sorted out a scooter
So I can do it by myself
Not needing you to push me
I don't like accepting help

There I've said it
The one thing I really fear
The thing I dread more than anything
Why I stopped showing I care

Relying on, needing help
Not being my own boss
Letting you take charge for once
The ultimate loss

Now I know, Will I be able to
Not be an independent me
Can I accept help, not be myself
We'll just have to wait and see.

Understanding
the question

I've just understood the question
You have been repeatedly asking
Why has it taken me so long?
Why have I just started listening?

It's like the light bulbs just come on
How stupid can I be?
I now know what you're saying
You're asking "do you love or need me"

It's not about my illness
It's not about the kids
It's about me
And how much, to you, I give

Cooking cleaning
Making tea
Washing hoovering
Doing the laundry

That's not showing how much you feel
Why haven't I seen that before?
I used to laugh and enjoy myself
That's when I showed you more

We've both been angry
and we've got upset
Lots have been said
And I've taken on debt

But now I know the question
At last I can see
Why don't I know the answer to?
"Why can't you show you love me?"

You made my heart sing

From day one
You made my heart sing
You spoiled me
I was your everything

You moved heaven and earth
To be with me
What you gave up
No one could see

When we're back here
I realise
Cos I feel it in your heart
And I see it in your eyes

What we put you through
How we made you feel
Hearing you say that
Makes me reel

I have got to stop
Making it all about me
Because now somehow
Parkinson's is all I can see

But I'm more than that
There's more to me
I need to buck up
Then hopefully

I will see you smile
And make your heart sing
I want you to feel loved
And know you're my everything

So once again
I'm asking for your help
To get me back
And once again the master of my health

We knew it wasn't going to be easy

We knew it wasn't going to be easy
There was a lot we couldn't foresee
But we took the plunge anyway
And you decided to live with me

It was a whirlwind to begin with
The benefits clear as day
My health improved so much
The doctors put the credit your way

But there were also difficult times
I go right into myself
Shutting you out completely
Worrying about my health

Don't dwell, don't worry about it
It's bloody easy to say
Only the ignorant say these things
So they can confidently walk away

Otherwise they'd have to listen
To take time out and hear
To give up precious time from their schedule
And help you with this fear

I wish I could explain
Even get you to see
But I see that'll never happen
And know that one day you will flee

Don't bear a grudge
And won't hold this against you
As none of us had any idea
We just hadn't got a clue

I wish it could be perfect
I wish I could once again be me
I'd love to enjoy living again
And enjoy every minute completely

I know if I can't
It will be such a waste
Cos life's not a dress rehearsal
So I need to make haste

And go back to taking chances
And not thinking what tomorrow could bring
Cos that won't stop it happening
Or take away the sting

This past week has shown me
At the end I will stand alone
Not because I have too
But because I need to atone

I hear my loved ones say
I will look after you
But there's no way I'll let this occur
Because I won't put them through

Helping me and struggling to care
Knowing what trouble it'll mean
I'll put myself in a care home
Cos of what in my life I've seen

When I can't do what I want
Before I'll rely on my family
I'll choose this way out you see
As a burden I'm determined not to be.

You're struggling with your emotions

You're struggling with your emotions
And I can understand why
Cos with my illness I'm not easy
Especially at nights when I cry.

Or when I wake up screaming
Cos the night terrors are back again
I thought I'd learned to control them
But they're appearing every night the same

Me myself and I
That's what I've become
Never giving you attention
Cos I obsess at being a mum

Wandering at night
And sitting doing art
A solo life I've slipped into
I can see why you want to part

Oh what do I do
How can I be fair to you
Do I let you go
Or hang on and see it through

I know I love you
And to say goodbye
Would totally destroy me
And rivers I would cry

This amount of trauma
And all the stress
Would destroy me
And bring on the end no less

But is it fair
To hold on to us
Just to save myself
As without you I'm dust

Is it time
Is the end here
At this moment I am tired
I'm not sure I care

About going on
I'm tempted to give in
To put my arms down
And let Parkinson's win

The fights getting too hard
Is it time to call it a day
Do I give in now
And just gently float away

But then, there
Somewhere deep inside
I can feel my babies smile
And I can hear them cry

That's what keeps me going
that's what forces me to go on
whatever happens, happens
But I will get over it and out will come the sun.

Why can't you sleep?

Why can't you sleep
What's the matter with you
Just close your eyes
And do what I do

It's easy to say
And easy to judge
Until you've got thoughts in your head
That you just cannot budge

It's only at night
When it's quiet and still
That my mind starts to think
And I remember I'm ill

During the day
I do not have time
But in the small hours
It's always on my mind

You cannot imagine
The terror that I feel
When I let myself dwell
On things I usually try not to deal

I struggle so much now
In such a short time
It scares me to death
How quickly I've declined

I can calculate
At this rapid pace
At best 2 more years
Then I'll have to face

The end of my freedom
To do what I want
A future of uncertainty
My mind it does haunt

How bad will it be
How hard will it get
Will I manage to cope
It really makes me fret

It's easy for you
It's easy to sleep
When you don't have deal
With the thoughts that I have to keep

Roll on the morning
Come on day break
I'm glad when it comes around
And I can get up and wake

Soon my babies will be here
And the torturous night will end
And the dark thoughts that haunted me
Will disappear and I'll start again

Many, many years ago

You have to understand
Many, many years ago
When I was a child
There's something you must know

It was a very abusive time
And not one you could ever forget
It left lots of very deep scars
That's why shouting makes me so upset

I will not end my days
In the same way they began
Scared and afraid
Because of a bad tempered old man

And I will not allow
And cannot tolerate
Seeing my grandchildren crying
So think before it's too late

Apologise now,
This can't happen again
you have to understand
You should be ashamed

I am the person I am now
Because of what I went through
And I cannot change that
Not even for you

I am disabled
I am chronicle Ill
I'll only get worse
There's no magic pill

I wet myself now
Wait till it's the bed
If your comments are cruel now
Will you wish I was dead

You have no patience
You're not tolerant or kind
How will you cope
When I mess my behind

Your heads in the sand
You need to wise up
Get real John
Take a close look

I am what I am

I am what I am
That's not going to change
Obviously caring
Is not really your game

I carefully adjust my smile
Each and every day
To make it look authentic
In each and every way

If it looks convincing
And I get it on just right
No one will suspect
That I'm starting to lose my fight

I can't control the pain
And I'm struggling to walk
Sometimes I find it hard
To hold my knife and fork

Help I pray each day
To hide my embarrassment
Since finding myself suffering
incontinence

No feeling in my hands
I'm struggling to grip
I forget to pick my feet up
And have now started to trip

Medications are taking over
There is no room for slack
They're all so highly addictive
It's too late. No turning back

Depression is my enemy
Anxiety and fear
At war with my emotions
Something I dare not share

Now God it's time to hold my hand
And walk here by my side
Because there is only you now
To which I can confide

Lord give me self-belief
and make it all make sense
Help me accept what the future holds
and maintain my confidence.

I have to take it day by day
and not let anyone know
How difficult it is to find that smile
And not to let my fear show.

I know the exact time when things changed and a more positive me reappeared. My daughter and her family went on holiday and I was twiddling my thumbs a bit. Then a dear friend split from her husband and needed help. I found helping her and listening to her talk about how she felt, actually helped me. She was struggling with her husband, as he is disabled and depressed, made me realise John's point of view, about our problems.

She's up early
every morning

She's up early every morning
Just popping for a cuppa tea
I saw the light as I was jogging
And I was passing by you see

At night in her pyjama's
And her Woolley hat
Just checking you were ok
Or I nipped in for a chat

She rings for an hour
At least 3 times a day
Everyone's surprised
We've always got something to say

Not that I am moaning
As I love her very much
I know I am so lucky
Her devotion can't be touched

I don't like to see her worry
Or watch her wear herself out
With a job and 2 young children
She's always dashing about

So make the most of going away
Relax and take time out
Sit for once, chill and, relax
Let everyone else run about

And no need to worry
About me and stress
I'll make sure I'm careful
And I'll make sure to rest

Happy holiday
Hip hip hip hooray
Jamaica beware
Cos the Smith's are on their way.

Looking in the mirror

I look in the mirror
Who is looking back at me
I do not recognize
The image that I see

Where is all the fight
Where is all the strength
Where is the determined pain
Who'd go to any length

For a while I thought I'd lost her
Mrs I won't give in
Thank goodness she's returned
Cos I need her to win

She is the warrior
She will always fight
She has never given in
Because she's always right

She will get on your nerves
She doesn't know when to stop
But I wouldn't be without her
I now need her quite a lot

But this time she took some finding
I'd looked almost everywhere
And then a friend needed help
And all of a sudden she appeared

Now once again I can do battle
Parkinson's I know you will always win
But it won't be today
Cos I've found me again

This time it took some months of struggling with myself, to not give in and to come back fighting again. It gets harder and harder to find the strength to pull myself out of the pit of despair at times.

Me and John started to understand each other a bit more and started talking properly and more importantly listening again. We started to get stronger again and I am now trying to work on getting fitter and losing weight, to see how if this helps my knees and improves my mobility!!! Watch this space.

What am I to do?

What am I to do?
Do I listen to all the voices?
Is it time to give in?
Is it time to accept defeat?
And admit I can no longer win.

It is the moment I have dreaded
And now it looks like it's here
I am rapidly losing my mobility
And am facing a wheelchair

The struggle is too much
The pain too hard to bear
But can I now accept this?
Why does this seem unfair?

So far I've been able to ignore
And pretend that I am alright
But now all of a sudden
This became a serious fight

Every loss is massive
Every defeat hurts more
But I have to remain mentally strong
To keep ahead in this war

But my stubbornness is hurting
The ones I hold so dear
So it's time to stop being stupid
And face one more fear

It's time to count my blessings
And be grateful I'm still here
It's not about giving up
It's accepting the help that's there

This illness isn't easy
It takes you piece by piece
The strength is in acceptance
And doing it with grace

Of course I'm afraid
Who wouldn't be?
But at the end of the day
I'm alive and I'm still me

I did something I promised myself I'd never do

I did something I promised myself I'd never do
I looked at the Parkinson's scale to check how
far I was through

I've moved on to phase 3, now I'm exactly halfway
A sobering thought as it only seemed like yesterday

When I got the news, the diagnosis
After 4 long years, a worrying prognosis

That was 6 years ago, so I estimate
At best I've got 10, but it'll be more like 8.

Now it gets tough, will I be able to cope
Or will I just give in, lay down and mope

Now these past months of ups and down's,
have now left me so unsure
I wonder if John's feet touch the ground
As he runs of out of that door

Do I end it now and hope for the best
But I am very sure, I can overcome this test

It'll knock me back, there is no doubt
But his moaning and bitching is wearing me out

My kids, home and my job are important to me
I take pride in the success I've had with all three

I'm not saying everyone should be the same
Your life's goals are yours to set, it's an individual game

John is so used to, putting himself first
And this is what he's done, from the day his mum gave birth

He has no home, nothing that's his
I just couldn't cope with a life like this

He does work hard, so he can enjoy himself
And there's nothing wrong with that, if you have your health

No one's right and no one's wrong
Were all different, our bands just play a different song

But I can't change and put myself first
I just couldn't live with all that hurt

If there's something that I want, then I will go to work
This way then I'm the only person, the only one who will get hurt.

I may be stupid, I may not be right
But I'll be able to live with my conscience and sleep very well at night

So do I end it now? Is it time to say goodbye
Or do I hang on to something, that now feels like a lie

When you're chronically ill

When you're chronically ill
And the sands of time start to run low
When you're scared and afraid
As life's light fails to glow

When deaths by your side
Holding your hand
And the pain is getting too much
That you can hardly stand

You reach out your arms
And pray with your heart
You hold your loved ones close
Because you know you'll soon part

When all that you know
It's what you've always done
So you continue to work
And play with your grandchildren in the Sun

But every day is a struggle
Every step it gets harder
Hope this new longer there
And it's starting to get darker

It's at this dark hour
You know what you're worth
When you know you'll soon be back
To just being earth

Will it be heaven or hell?
Is there such a thing
Does God really exist?
Do angels really sing?

Will loved ones cope?
How long will they cry?
Will they be looked after?
When it's my time to die

These thoughts do you keep
When you're chronically ill
Especially at night
When everything is still

So God here my prayers
And comfort my mind
Hold me till morning
And leave the long night behind

Help me manage my fear
As I try not to be afraid
Of when the day comes
That loved ones standby in my grave

So often I cry
And look into the sky
Please don't take me yet
I'm not ready to die.

The Darkness

Darkness is slowly returning
Horror will soon reign
The night terrors wait in the shadows
Fear lays beside me again

I pull the quilt up high
And curl up in a ball
I can feel the day's medications running out
Now I've little protection at all

Soon the hour I dread
I slowly drift off to sleep
Time for past events
From my subconscious now to creep

Now this evil has a grip
It has a hold over me
There's nothing I can do
Only death will set me free

Bird song breaks the curse
Morning slowly dawns
I uncurl my legs out slowly
Stretching my arms up and yawn

Why do you get up early?
Why don't you stay in bed?
Swap places for an evening
Live one night in my head

And you will understand
You will see clearly why
I am relieved when morning comes
And I can wave the night goodbye

The Sands of Time

The Sands of time run very quickly
All too soon loved ones have to go
We're then parted by the greatest mystery
What happens next we do not know

All we really can know for sure
Is loved ones are missed and grief is forever more

The pain of being parted is sometimes too
much to take
The grief and the loneliness makes your
fragile heart ache

Time does not heal
You still miss them everyday
But somehow you learn to live with this pain in a way

Soon the tears start to slow
And Memories in your heart then leave a glow

That's when you realise, they'll always be there
While you are able to remember. All the love
you once shared

I open my eyes

I open my eyes
Each and every day
Wondering how I'm going to cope
Feeling this way

It would be so easy
Just to give in
Just to stay in my bed
And let Parkinson's win

Then I hear the door go
And I see those lovely smiles
And I realise what drives me
To go that extra mile

My reason to live
My reason to survive
My driving force
It's for them that I strive

I want them to remember
To love and admire
A woman of courage
With a driving desire

Not a miserable old sod
Not a self-pitying person
But a fighter, a hero
Someone determined to go on

Someone who'll never give in
Someone who'll always be there
To shape and to guide them
And show them that I care

I want to inspire
I want to impress
I want to encourage them
To be the very best

The very best they can be
And to accept nothing less
And make sure they enjoy
Every day that they are blessed

Don't waste a minute
Of the precious time that you have
Enjoy your life now
And one day you will be glad

You get only one chance
Just this one time to give
It's not a dress rehearsal
So go on, do it and live

I wrote the last lot of poems, during many months of struggling with depression and myself. I was trying not to give in and searching harder than ever before to find the inner strength, to climb out of the pit of despair, I found myself in.

I was struggling with the unbearable pain in my knees, pain I never could have imagined my self being able to live with.

This was my darkest period ever, even I doubted my own strength and ability to rise from the ashes, like the Phoenix.

I had lost my motivation, strength, everything, well almost everything! Two little lights shone brightly and they led me back from the darkness, to sanity once again, my girls. I took week off in the summer holidays just to spend with them and, well I'll let you read on and see what happened next.

Me and John have never been stronger and funnily enough it was writing this book that helped me. It reminded me of all the love I have and am surround by, at home and at work and it reminded me what is really important.

"LIFE"

I am sick of the self-pity

I am sick of the self-pity that I now wallow in
If it were bloody possible, then I'd whip me for that sin

Get a bloody grip, stand up now and fight
Stop being a snivelling wretch, there's no way that is right

Where do I go for help, I turn to my warrior queen
"I've been expecting you she said"' are you ready to be seen?"

Then come on, let's not delay, I will show you how
All the power I have learned, I will use on you now

I cannot help you win, but you're knees I'll help to mend
Parkinson's will have its day, but eye to eye once more you'll stand

It will take over bit by bit, you'll lose a little at a time
But I refuse to surrender, my dignity this will be forever mine

I will never give that up, I wasn't born to give in
I was born a survivor, I only know how to win

Once more I pull on my armour, my sword and shield held high
I gather up my foot soldiers, come on Himmy,
I need you once more to fly.

I'd like to say "thank-you" to all at the NUH Parkinson's re-ablement team at the City Hospital. Especially my "Warrior Queen" Christine.

My Granddaughters

Those smiles, those faces, true beauty, no heirs, no graces
It's always been a love I could never explain
They inspire me to overcome my troubles and chronic pain
They give me life, yet I was a part of creating theirs
Their dedication, the love they show and freely share
I rely on and exist, the reason I'm still alive
Is the fun, the memories, the courage, the drive
To always be there, to love and look out for
My angels, my life, my granddaughters that I adore

Love

Loves first flush
Oh I love you
Once so exciting
Once so new

This luxury
This happiness
Was soon replaced
With a seriousness

Because I was ill
We soon realised
I needed you here
Close by my side

You gave up your life
Moved across the country
You took on the role
Of caring for me

Even though at times
I showed no gratitude
One Minute I was loving
The next in a mood

The night terrors were a shock
Screaming in fright
Waking you up
At all times of night

But you learned to adapt
But at quite a cost
You had a haemorrhic stroke
And I thought you were lost

In these past few years
You've managed to cram
A life time of excitement
Not bad for an old man

Nights out and holidays
Romance ever after
Not a minute has been wasted
We've had our share of arguments and laughter

We've watched the sun rise
In different parts of the world
Sailed on the ocean
You're a man of your word

You took on the unknown
And stood firmly by my side
Fought an enemy you couldn't see
And it's been one hell of a ride

I am now aware
Those first innocent words we say
Didn't mean then
What they now mean today

Because love is a journey
And a difficult one
Not something to say lightly
Or to say just for fun

It's not a medal
It's not a badge
It's something you earn
Through good times and through bad

Himmy you've stood by
And kept your promise to me
And now I couldn't imagine
Without you, where I'd be

So now I can say
With all certainty
How much I love you
And know how much you love me

That terrible 4 letter word

I went to see my physio
And a 4 letter word she uttered

You can't say that word to me
I'm speechless, devastated, gutted

I've never heard anything so disgusting
I said abruptly and out loud

Have I ever done anything to hurt you?
No! I have always been honest and proud

She did not get flustered
And was very matter-of-fact

When I stood on the scale
And she said that I was fat

Then she spoke that word
And everywhere went quiet

It no good avoiding it
You now need to diet

Counting calories

I am counting calories and it's very, very tough
because 1 square of chocolate, isn't nearly enough

Everything I love, everything I adore
Are always so full of calories, I can't have them any more

Crisps and chocolate cake, cream buns and apple pie
Smothered in chocolate ice cream, just a taste I'd like to try

Fish and chips or pizza, I now have to say no
And over to the salad bar for rabbit food I now go

I could have a chocolate bar, if I ate nothing else all day
And a hot chocolate fudge cake, well that would be 2 days I'd say

But on a more positive note, my weight is going down
Even if my face, does nothing now but frown

Another bonus to, is my maths is getting better
All this to lose weight and help me to get fitter

I know it's not been long

I know it's not been long, but I'm managing to lose weight
A little bit of exercise, it seems my goal at last I might make

I'm a little bit excited and a little bit afraid
I dare not build my hope up, this mistake in the past I've made

I'm not expecting a miracle, I know there's no magic wand
But everything seems on track again, we've rekindled our bond

We've had our ups and downs, our arguments and frowns
Sometimes it gets tough and we say enough, is enough

But something binds us together, we just can't turn and walk away
Neither able to wave good bye and say "I'm calling it a day"

I'm sure we'll have a lot more hills, to face and climb up and down
For we now appreciate the good times more and refuse to wear a frown

I think it might be true, in fact I'm positive it is
We feel it when we hug and especially when we kiss

A sense of belonging, of trust and security
This really is true love, between my Himmy Bear and me

Your ill, Take it easy

Your ill, Take it easy
Sit down, rest your knees
Accept your limitations
Really, please

Don't they know me?
They should by now
Take it easy
I don't know how

A wheelchair
Don't make me smile
Bring one near
And I'll run a mile

I have a week off
With T & Zu
Sit in doors
With nothing to do

Not bloody likely
I'm off out
I want to hear them
Laugh and shout

Run around
Having some fun
Eating picnics
In the sun

Monday Ice skating
Falling down
Shaky legs
And a few frowns

But quick as that
Confidence grows
Flushed cheeks
And a bright red nose

Skating round
Holding the wall
They soon improve
And have a ball

Tired out
Off we go
By the river
Nice and slow

Chilling out
Eating snacks
Laughing and joking
When the geese attack

A game of tennis
Then a little walk
Around the pond
We chat and talk

Then a slow ride home
And talk about our day
Then a chippy tea
And on our iPads we play

Time for bed
2 tired little girls
Dream sweet dreams
My angels on earth

More plans a foot
Tomorrow is another day
More adventures
To come our way

Click and climb
Then to the park
Sitting up late
And laughing till dark

Then off into Sherwood
The forest no less
Safety gear on
Going racing, no stress

In a go-cart
Fast round the track
Oh what a buzz
No looking back

3 days of fun
It's been such a blast
But you're ill they say
And you know it can't last

But if it's so bad
And not good for me
Why now do I feel?
So alive and so free

You cannot comprehend

You cannot comprehend
The battle I have to fight
It will never be won
with weapons or with might

I have already accepted
The physical war is lost
It took time to come to terms with this
And at a heavy cost

I've already seen those fighting
A similar battle you see
Fall already and give up
What you ask is the difference with me

I am too bloody minded
This is how I've always been
Right back to before I was born
My tenacity was seen

I have fought all my life
I don't know any other way
I know I'm not always right
I understand what you are trying to say

I won't accept a wheelchair
I will not give up work
I will spoil my children
No matter how much it hurts

Parkinson's will have its day
But it will be when I decide
Because like my mother before
I choose the day I die

It is in my DNA
It is everything I am
And this dreaded illness
Can try everything it can

Because mentally I will never be beat
I am stubborn and I am strong
I cannot change me now
Not for my family, you, or anyone

Watch me reclaim
my title back

All you see is some old lady
And a disabled one at that
Now see a master in action
Watch me reclaim my title back

I will not fight fairly
I will not fight face to face
I will use every dirty tactic
Even if I have to be embarrassed and disgraced

Watch me stretch out my wings
Watch the dragon take off and fly
Watch me soar again
Watch me once more rule the sky

Stand back and see
Look on and admire
As I take on Parkinson's
And incinerate it with fire

You are now my chosen ones
The ones who will succeed me
My babies, two strong women
I will train you how to be

But you have to trust me
And know I have your back
You have to have faith, more than ever before
Never doubt me, be afraid, or slack

As hand in hand together
Girls you and I now have to fight
And we will win and overcome
Because with you, I know I'll be alright

Every path is different

As you travel along life's journey
No two roads are ever the same
Not everyone has a tree lined Avenue
Or a countryside Lane

Some walk along dark Alleys
And some hit a dead end or two
For some it's all uphill
And some all built up with no view

There's no method, no plan, no race
No reason, no punishment to face
You're placed on the road just by chance
And it's up to you to divert and enhance

All Roads lead to the same place
If you don't get distracted along the way
Make the best of the journey no matter what
And try and keep dark thoughts at bay

Sometimes life doesn't seem fair
Some seem to have such a lot
Others seem to suffer so much
The secret is to be happy with what you've got

Make the most of each day
That you're gifted with life
And never take anything for granted

On the right road you stay
Try not to go the wrong way
Always be happy and contented

Whatever we suffer, is a trial just down here
Eternity will be oh so sweet

This is not forever, Just a blink of an eye
And your suffering will make forever a treat

Will I be famous?

Will I be famous?
Will I have my day?
Or will this come to nothing
And will I just fade away?

Will anyone be bothered?
Will anyone really care?
Will they really want to?
Get inside my head and share

My thoughts and experiences
My life wrote in poetry
Are they really interested?
In the person that is me

Do they want to know?
What goes on inside my head?
Perhaps they will one day
When I am long gone and dead

Do I want everyone?
Everyone I know
To know how afraid I get
The dark thoughts I dare not show

Would you like to visit?
Spend a while inside my head?
Get to feel the madness
My nightmares can now be read

A childhood of abuse
Beatings and the terror
The darkenss I have to come to terms with
My faults, my weaknesses my errors

All there written down
For all the world to see
My journey with Parkinson's
Everything private about me

Do I want my day?
Do I want to share?
Is the world ready yet?
For my story now to hear

9 781912 694648